$16.95

The Underground Railroad

by Ann Heinrichs

Content Adviser: Professor Sherry L. Field,
Department of Social Science Education, College of Education,
The University of Georgia

Reading Adviser: Dr. Linda D. Labbo,
Department of Reading Education, College of Education,
The University of Georgia

COMPASS POINT BOOKS

Minneapolis, Minnesota

Compass Point Books
3109 West 50th Street, #115
Minneapolis, MN 55410

Visit Compass Point Books on the Internet at *www.compasspointbooks.com* or e-mail your request
to *custserv@compasspointbooks.com*

Photographs ©: North Wind Picture Archives, cover, 10, 16, 31, 37; Schomburg Center for
Research in Black Culture, The New York Public Library, 4, 13, 18; Unicorn Stock Photos/Andre
Jenny, 5; Hulton Getty/Archive Photos, 7; Unicorn Stock Photos/Aneal Vohra, 8; Stock Montage,
9, 14, 33; Unicorn Stock Photos/Jim Shippee, 11; Archive Photos, 12, 15, 19, 20, 27, 34, 39;
Library of Congress, 17, 21, 23, 38, 40; The Newberry Library/Stock Montage, 25; XNR
Productions, Inc., 29.

Editors: E. Russell Primm and Emily J. Dolbear
Photo Researcher: Svetlana Zhurkina
Photo Selector: Linda S. Koutris
Designer: Bradfordesign, Inc.

Library of Congress Cataloging-in-Publication Data

Heinrichs, Ann.
   The Underground Railroad / by Ann Heinrichs.
     p. cm. — (We the people)
   Includes bibliographical references and index.
   ISBN 0-7565-0102-4 (lib. bdg.)
    1. Underground railroad—Juvenile literature. 2. Fugitive slaves—United States—History—
19th century—Juvenile literature. [1. Underground railroad. 2. Fugitive slaves.] I. Title. II. We the
people (Compass Point Books)
   E450 .H49 2001
   973.7'115—dc21
                                                            00-011020

TABLE OF CONTENTS

"Follow the Drinking Gourd"

Follow the drinking gourd,

Follow the drinking gourd,

For the old man is waiting for to carry you to freedom

If you follow the drinking gourd.

Before the Underground Railroad, slaves set out alone on their flight to freedom.

Slave labor allowed the South to run huge cotton plantations like this one.

This was a song of hope for thousands of runaway slaves. Once they escaped, they were running for their lives. And "north" was the way to run.

The "drinking **gourd**" was the Big Dipper. This is a group of seven stars in the night sky that looks like a long-handled drinking cup, or dipper.

5

Two of those stars are the "pointer stars." They point directly to the bright North Star. For runaways, or **fugitives**, that star was their guide to freedom.

Slaves learned the song from a one-legged sailor named Peg Leg Joe. This old man worked at odd jobs on **plantations** in the South. Secretly, he made friends with slaves and taught them the song. Hidden in the words were secret codes: "When the sun comes back and the first quail calls. . . . The river ends between two hills. . . . When the great big river meets the little river. . . ." They were directions for the road to freedom on the Underground Railroad.

THE RAILROAD WITH NO TRACKS

The Underground Railroad was not a real railroad. It didn't have train cars, tracks, or a schedule. Yet thousands of people traveled to freedom on this train. The Underground Railroad was a secret **network** of people who operated in the dark of

Harriet Tubman (far left) was a leader of the Underground Railroad.

7

This site in Albany, Kansas, was a stop on the Underground Railroad.

night. Their mission was a dangerous one—to help African-Americans escape from slavery in the Southern states.

People used the language of railroads to keep their work secret. The people who led escaping slaves on a safe journey were called "conductors." "Agents" hid runaways and gave them food and clothes. "Stations" on the railroad were houses where runaways would be safe. The runaways themselves were called "passengers" or "**freight**." Using these terms, people could talk about the Underground Railroad and seem to be having a normal chat about train rides.

$200 REWARD!

RANAWAY from the subscriber, living near Upper Marlboro', Prince George's County, Md., on the 22d of Sept., 1861, my negro man JOHN, who calls himself *JOHN LEE*. He is 24 years old, a little below the ordinary height, well built; has a remarkable fine set of teeth, which he shows when talking, and of very smiling countenance. Said negro was hired at the time he left to Mr. John A. Frasier, in Surratts District. Also, my negro man ANDREW, who calls himself *ANDREW AMBUSH*. He ran-away on the 1st of January, 1862. He is about 23 years old, tall and slender built, quite black, long thick lips, full suit of hair

I will give the above reward for the apprehension of said negroes, or $100 for either of them, provided they are delivered to me or secured in jail, so that I get them again.

WILLIAM P. PUMPHREY.

Welwood, Jan. 22, 1862.

Advertisements offered large rewards for returning escaped slaves.

The Underground Railroad was dangerous for the slaves and their helpers. Runaways who were caught could be bitten by dogs or shot. If they were caught, the slaves were dragged back to their masters and cruelly beaten, even hanged. Anyone who hid slaves or helped them escape faced time in jail.

Runaway slaves who were caught and returned to their owners received cruel punishments.

The Declaration of Independence states that every human being has certain rights.

In spite of the dangers, as many as 100,000 slaves rode the Underground Railroad to freedom in the North. More than 3,000 "railroad workers" helped any way that they could. Some drove wagons or boats with people hidden inside. Others hid **escapees** in their homes until it was safe for them to move on. Many others offered food, clothing, money, or just simple kindness.

One and all, they believed in the words of the Declaration of Independence. They believed that every human being is born with the right to "life, liberty, and the pursuit of happiness."

HOW IT ALL BEGAN

The Underground Railroad carried the most passengers between 1830 and 1860, but slaves had been trying to escape as early as the 1500s. That's when **colonists** from Spain began settling the islands off North America's southeastern coast. The Spaniards bought men, women, and children

This Dutch ship brought twenty African slaves to Jamestown, Virginia, in 1619.

Slave traders kidnapped men, women, and children in Africa and forced them onto ships bound for North America.

kidnapped from Africa. They forced these kidnapped people to work as slaves on their plantations. From the beginning, slaves risked their lives to escape.

13

Soon, English colonists began settling the mainland of North America. After the American Revolution (1775–1783), the thirteen colonies became the United States of America.

People in the northern and southern United States had very different ways of life. Northern states relied on manufacturing and trade. Southerners depended on crops such as cotton. Their huge plantations needed slave labor to

Work on cotton plantations was backbreaking.

14

In public squares, slaves were sold to the highest bidder.

produce the cotton. Slave traders brought shiploads of Africans to sell to the Southern planters.

Their owners thought of slaves as property. And they were worth a lot of money. Healthy men or women were sold for $1,000 each. But the law granted slave owners even more power over their slaves. A Virginia law allowed owners to "kill and destroy" runaways.

15

Some owners treated their slaves kindly. Other owners treated them as less than human. Slaves worked the fields from sunup till sundown. They were poorly fed and lived in rundown shacks. Anyone who disobeyed or worked too slowly might be beaten, whipped, or chained.

Slave cabins had few comforts.

16

Slaves were often separated from their children.

Most heartbreaking of all were the slave sales. Families were often ripped apart. A husband, his wife, and their children might be sold to three different masters. No wonder the slaves dreamed of being free.

As soon as escaped slaves reached the North, they were free.

The Fugitive Slave Act of 1793 allowed slave owners to capture runaways. By this time, however, most Northern states had outlawed slavery. Once a slave reached the North, he or she was safe. Now the stage was set. Before long, the Underground Railroad would be up and rolling!

18

THE ABOLITIONIST MOVEMENT: LAYING THE GROUNDWORK

As time went on, more and more Northerners spoke out against slavery. They were called **abolitionists**—people who wanted the whole nation to get rid of slavery.

Not all abolitionists agreed about how and why to free the slaves. Some, such as William Lloyd Garrison, wanted all slaves to be freed immediately. Others preferred to move slowly.

William Lloyd Garrison

19

Frederick Douglass

Many were against slavery for religious reasons. They believed that God created all people as equals. Some abolitionists showed up at slave sales and bought as many slaves as they could. Then they cared for them until they could move them into a free state.

One of America's greatest abolitionists was Frederick Douglass. He escaped from slavery in Maryland in 1838. Then Douglass founded an African-American newspaper called the *North Star*. He also wrote several books about his years as a slave. Douglass's fiery speeches against slavery inspired hundreds of others to join the fight.

20

Harriet Beecher Stowe was another famous abolitionist. Her book *Uncle Tom's Cabin* opened people's eyes to the horrors of slavery. Stowe showed her readers that slavery was about right and wrong—not about property or politics.

Harriet Beecher Stowe

The Fugitive Slave Act of 1850 made things harder than ever. It allowed slave hunters to follow runaways into the Northern free states and bring them back to the South. Now the only safe place to run was Canada, beyond America's northern border.

LIFE ON THE RUN

In Africa, it was the people's custom to pass news along through songs. Slaves in the South used songs to send information, too. In the fields, work songs contained secret messages about escape plans. "Follow the Drinking Gourd," for example, told slaves how to escape from Alabama and Mississippi.

For a runaway slave, day-to-day life was a nightmare. Fugitives could travel only at night, and then only for a few hours. Their map was the night sky, where the North Star pointed their way. At every step, they held their breath and listened for the bark of **bloodhounds** in the night. On and on they ran, through twigs and thorns that ripped their clothes and skin.

22

"The Fugitive's Song" is an abolitionist song written by Frederick Douglass, who was himself a runaway slave.

By day, they hid out in woods, hills, or swamps. If slave hunters were on their trail, life became even more desperate. A group of runaways might have to scatter, with family members losing

23

track of one another. And no slave hunter left home without his gun. He would shoot to injure, not kill, a fugitive because a slave was worth money. But plenty of "accidents" happened, and many fugitives died from a gunshot in the back.

Most runaways were men. Life on the run was harder and more dangerous for women and children. Once a man reached freedom, he could work and save money. Then he might help his family escape or buy their freedom.

Conductors and agents kept each other up to date if they had spotted slave hunters nearby. They often used secret signals. A lantern swinging in front of a safe house meant, "Come on—the coast is clear!"

Slaves would do almost anything to escape. Several fugitives might hide in a wagonload of

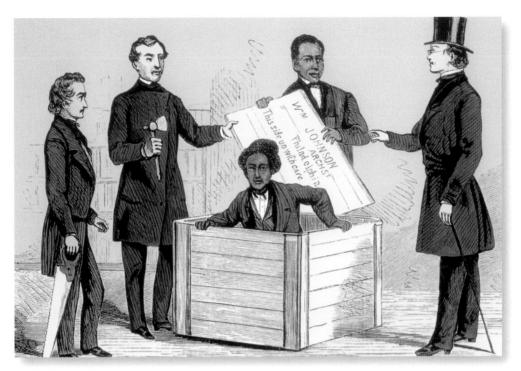

Henry "Box" Brown asked friends to ship him to Pennsylvania in a box!

grain sacks under the crushing weight of the grain. But Henry "Box" Brown went further still.

Henry had some friends put him into a wooden box and nail it shut. Following Brown's directions, they shipped the box to Philadelphia, Pennsylvania. It was a rough trip, but Henry arrived in one piece—alive and free!

THE TALE OF ELIZA

Anyone who has read *Uncle Tom's Cabin* will never forget the heartbreaking tale of a runaway named Eliza.

Eliza had learned that her master planned to sell her little boy the very next day. She had to escape that night or lose her child forever. It was a cold winter night, but Eliza did what she had to do—run! At last, with a search party close behind her, Eliza reached the Ohio River. She knew she would rather drown than be caught.

Her child clasped in her arms, Eliza stepped onto a floating sheet of ice. As one chunk of ice sank under her weight, she sprang to another one, and then another. Sometimes she fell into the icy

An advertisement for Uncle Tom's Cabin, *Harriet Beecher Stowe's antislavery book*

water. Then she placed her little boy on the next chunk of ice and carefully pulled herself up onto it.

Worn-out and half frozen, Eliza at last dragged herself and her child onto the shore. Kindly people helped her from one Underground Railroad station to another. At last, she was able to reach freedom and safety in Canada.

WHERE THE RAILROAD RAN

The Underground Railroad ran along two main routes. Slaves from the southeastern United States took the eastern line. By land or sea, they headed for states on the northeast coast.

Philadelphia became an important port for boatloads of runaways. From there, some moved north into the state of New York. They headed for the cities of Rochester or Niagara, near Lake Ontario. Then they had only to cross the lake into Canada. Others went to Vermont, which shared a land border with Canada.

Slaves who lived far from the coast took another route. By land, they ran north toward the

CANADA

North Dakota
Minnesota
South Dakota
Nebraska
Kansas
Oklahoma
Texas

Lake Superior
Michigan
Wisconsin
St. Paul
Iowa
Missouri
Missouri
Arkansas
Louisiana

Lake Michigan
Lake Huron
Detroit
Sandusky
Illinois
Ind.
Ohio
Ky.
Tennessee
Miss.
Alabama
Georgia

Niagara Falls
Lake Ontario
Lake Erie
Rochester
N.Y.
Penn.
Philadelphia
W. Va.
Va.
N.C.
S.C.

Hudson
Vt.
Maine
N.H.
Mass.
R.I.
Conn.
N.J.
Del.
Md.

Atlantic Ocean

General movement of escaped slaves

Florida

N

Gulf of Mexico

0   100   200   300 miles
0   100   200   300 kilometers

This map shows the Underground Railroad routes that slaves took from different areas.

29

mighty Ohio River. Once they crossed it into Ohio or Indiana, they could breathe a little easier. Along the north bank of the Ohio River lay entire towns that were against slavery. Runaways knew these spots well.

From Ohio, some went on to Detroit, Michigan. Only a narrow strip of water lay between Detroit and Canada. Others headed for Sandusky, Ohio, just across Lake Erie from Canada.

MEET SOME OF THE RAILROAD CREW

Underground Railroad workers belonged to all races and religions. Some of the bravest workers belonged to the Quaker religion—also known as

The Quakers worked bravely to help slaves find freedom.

the Society of Friends. The African Methodist Episcopal (AME) Church was also a powerful force for freedom.

Native Americans were part of the railroad, too. Since the earliest days of slavery, they had helped runaways to hide. They knew all the woods and swamps. Many escapees joined Native American families and married into Indian tribes.

Levi Coffin was the most famous agent on the railroad. He and his wife were religious Quakers in Newport (now Fountain City), Indiana. Once a band of slave hunters tried to question Coffin about some runaways. They found out so little, they decided that Coffin must be the president of the Underground Railroad.

Coffin was well known among slaves on the

run. Once they crossed the Ohio River, they were led to his two-story brick house. It was called the Grand Central Station of the Underground Railroad.

Levi Coffin

Between 1827 and 1847, Coffin helped more than 3,000 slaves escape. And he had a perfect record—not one of his fugitives was ever caught. One of his famous "guests" was Eliza Harris, whose story appears in *Uncle Tom's Cabin*.

Thomas Garrett

Thomas Garrett was a Quaker businessman in Wilmington, Delaware. He worked on the Underground Railroad for almost forty years. Once Garrett was arrested and fined $5,400 for his activities.

William Still, an African-American, was born free in the North. As a successful merchant in Philadelphia, he welcomed runaways into his home and gave them advice.

Another famous agent was John Rankin, a minister in Ripley, Ohio. A long stairway from the Ohio riverbank led up to his home. Slaves called it the Stairway to Freedom. Inside, Rankin and his family fed hundreds of escapees and hid them behind secret panels in the walls.

Harriet Beecher Stowe lived with the Rankins for a while. Many of the stories she heard there ended up in her book *Uncle Tom's Cabin*. A runaway named Josiah Henson was the real "Uncle Tom," and Eliza Harris was the real "Eliza."

THEY CALLED HER MOSES

Her name was Harriet Tubman, but people called her Moses. Like Moses in the Bible story, she led her people out of slavery to freedom in the Promised Land.

Harriet herself was born and raised a slave on a Maryland plantation. Once when she was thirteen, she tried to help a runaway slave. Her master hit her in the head with a rock and cracked her skull. For the rest of her life, she suffered from blackouts.

In 1849, Harriet escaped to the North. Then she resolved to help as many others as she could. In all, she made nineteen dangerous trips back to the South to lead slaves to safety.

Harriet was a master planner with a quick

mind. She made strict rules. There was to be "no foolish-ness" on the road. And no matter how hard the journey was, no one could turn back.

Harriet Tubman

Harriet carried a gun for safety, but it sometimes seemed she might use it to keep her passengers in line. Once a man began to grumble that he didn't want to go on. Harriet pulled out her gun and said, "Move or die!" He moved.

Harriet Tubman led more than 300 slaves to freedom—including her own elderly parents. Her track record on the Underground Railroad was perfect. As she said, "I never run my train off the track and I never lost a passenger."

THE RAILROAD CLOSES DOWN

Little by little, the differences between North and South were reaching the boiling point. In 1860, Southern states began to **secede** from the United States. They called themselves the Confederate States of America. In 1861, Confederates troops fired on U.S. troops, and the Civil War began.

On January 1, 1863, President Abraham Lincoln issued the Emancipation Proclamation. It declared that "all persons held as slaves within any

The Emancipation Proclamation

38

State . . . in rebellion against the United States shall be . . . forever free."

Slave owners, of course, did not rush to set their slaves free. But runaways knew they could now find safety behind the Union army's battle lines. After the Emancipation Proclamation, almost 179,000 African-Americans signed up as soldiers for the North.

Many African-Americans fought for the Union during the American Civil War.

President Abraham Lincoln was assassinated on April 14, 1865.

At last, on April 9, 1865, the war ended in victory for the North. Only five days later, President Lincoln was shot and killed. It was a tragic loss for the nation—and especially for those he had helped to free. But Lincoln's ideas lived on.

40

On December 6, 1865, Congress passed the Thirteenth Amendment to the Constitution. Once and for all, freedom was the law of the land: "Neither slavery nor involuntary servitude . . . shall exist within the United States." There would be no more need for an Underground Railroad.

Little by little, African-Americans took their place in American life. Some settled in the South, while others moved into the northern and western states. As they shared their talents and skills, they made life richer for all. They became doctors, lawyers, teachers, business owners, artists, writers, entertainers, and sports figures. Their labor helped build up the nation's powerful industries.

Best of all, they taught the nation a lesson it must never forget—that America is the land of the free and the home of the brave.

GLOSSARY

abolitionists—people who worked to get rid of slavery

bloodhounds—dogs trained to find a person by their sense of smell

colonists—people who settle in a new territory governed by their home country

escapees—people who have escaped

freight—goods shipped from one place to another

fugitives—runaways; people on the run from the law

gourd—the hard, round shell of the squash fruit

network—a group of people connected by the same interests

plantations—large farms that grow one main crop, such as cotton

secede—to withdraw

DID YOU KNOW?

- During the Civil War, Harriet Tubman worked for the Union army. She was a cook, a nurse, a scout, and a spy.

- Levi Coffin opened a store in Cincinnati, Ohio. Only goods made by people who were free were sold in his store.

- In 1870, the Fifteenth Amendment to the U.S. Constitution gave American men of all races the right to vote. But American women could not vote until 1920.

IMPORTANT DATES

Timeline

1793 — The nation's first Fugitive Slave Act is passed.

1850 — The U.S. Congress passes a harsher Fugitive Slave Act.

1852 — Harriet Beecher Stowe's *Uncle Tom's Cabin* is published.

1861 — The American Civil War begins.

1863 — President Abraham Lincoln issues the Emancipation Proclamation.

1865 — The Civil War ends; President Lincoln is assassinated; the Thirteenth Amendment outlaws slavery.

IMPORTANT PEOPLE

LEVI COFFIN

(1798–1877), *businessman in Fountain City, Indiana; said to be the leader of the Underground Railroad*

FREDERICK DOUGLASS

(1818–1895), *writer, newspaper publisher, and public speaker; former slave who became the leading African-American abolitionist of the 1800s*

JOHN RANKIN

(1793–1886), *Presbyterian minister whose home in Ripley, Ohio, was the most active Underground Railroad station*

HARRIET BEECHER STOWE

(1811–1896), *writer whose novel* Uncle Tom's Cabin *showed the horrors of slavery*

HARRIET TUBMAN

(1820?–1913), *former slave who became the most famous conductor on the Underground Railroad*

Want to Know More?

At the Library

Passaro, John. *Frederick Douglass: Journey to Freedom.* Chanhassen, Minn.:
Child's World, 1999.

Petry, Ann Lane. *Harriet Tubman: Conductor on the Underground Railroad.*
New York: HarperTrophy, 1996.

Winter, Jeanette. *Follow the Drinking Gourd.* New York: Knopf, 1992.

On the Web

National Geographic—The Underground Railroad
http://www.nationalgeographic.com/features/99/railroad/j1.html

For information on the Underground Railroad's routes, a timeline, and the
virtual journey of an escaped slave

The North Star Website
http://www.ugrr.org

For information on Underground Railroad safe houses, walking the
pathways of escapees and famous abolitionists

The Underground Railroad
http://education.ucdavis.edu/NEW/STC/lesson/socstud/railroad/contents.htm

For historical information, speeches by abolitionists, and stories told by
escaped slaves

Through the Mail

National Underground Railroad Freedom Center

312 Elm Street

20th floor

Cincinnati, OH 45202

877/648-4838

For information about this center that will open in 2003

On the Road

Levi Coffin House

113 U.S. 27 North

Fountain City, IN 47341

765/847-2432

To visit a real stop on the Underground Railroad

Rankin House

6152 Rankin Road

Ripley, OH 45167

937/392-1627

To see the most active Underground Railroad Station

INDEX

About the Author

Ann Heinrichs was born in Fort Smith, Arkansas. She began playing the piano at age three and thought she would grow up to be a pianist. Instead, she became a writer. Now she has written more than thirty-five books for children and young adults. Ann Heinrichs lives in Chicago, Illinois.